WHAT TO KNOW ABOUT

Concentrated Animal Feeding Operations

A CONSUMERS GUIDE TO MEAT CONSUMPTION

Pierre Mouchette

Real Property Experts LLC
an Environmental Knowledge Publication

CONCENTRATED ANIMAL FEEDING OPERATIONS

Copyright © 2020 by Pierre Mouchette
All rights reserved. No part of this publication may be reproduced or used in any manner without written permission of the Copyright Holder, except by a reviewer who may quote brief passages in a review.

First Edition: April 13, 2020
Real Property Experts LLC
Web Address: https://www.rpe4u.com
Contact: publications@rpe4u.com

Note: This publication comes in a variety of formats, such as Paperbacks and Electronic Books (e-books). Some material included with the paperback versions of this book may not be included in e-books, and vice versa.

Disclaimer: This Real Property Experts LLC (RPE) publication provides information about the subject matter covered. The author and publisher of this content are not acting as licensed professionals in the presentation of covered material and are not qualified to give advice normally provided by professionals in the fields of expertise of this content, nor are they responsible for errors and omissions. The information and statements made, are for educational purposes and are not intended to replace a one-on-one relationship with a qualified attorney, accountant, tax professional, or other licensed professionals. You are solely responsible for the use of any content and hold Real Property Experts LLC, its' subsidiary's and members harmless in any event or claim, demand, or damage, including reasonable attorneys' fees, asserted by any third party or arising out of your use of, or conduct on, articles and/or products.

RPE writers provide applicable content and break down complex topics so they are easier to understand. Information given may not apply to your specific situation, and products or services recommended may not be a good fit for your application While RPE strives to provide accurate up-to-date content, we cannot guarantee the accuracy and completeness of information provided. By using this content, you understand that all material is an expression of opinions and not professional advice.

RPE regularly updates articles, but it is possible that we may miss something. Use our content as a starting point before selecting to use and choose a service or product. The reader is advised to keep up to date on activities in their locale by consulting with the appropriate licensed professionals for decisions that could affect them.

CONCENTRATED ANIMAL FEEDING OPERATIONS

PREFACE

Concentrated Animal Feeding Operations (CAFOs) are livestock farms that operate at industrial factory levels. These operations can house anywhere from several hundred to millions of animals on one property, with most, focusing on chickens, hogs, beef cattle and dairy cows.

This book covers what you must know about the meats that are available at your local grocery or supermarket.

For comments on this publication please write to us at REAL PROPERTY EXPERTS LLC.

Pierre Mouchette, author

SPECIAL FEATURES

This book comes with a Website (https://www.synchronicity-investor.com)

THE SYNCHRONICITY INVESTOR website provides world class solutions for all. No matter if you are an individual, a small business owner, or a decision maker at a conglomerate, THE SYNCHRONICITY INVESTOR is committed to providing you with the information that you need to make informed decisions. We encourage you to think of THE SYNCHRONICITY INVESTOR as your go to source for knowledgeable information. Additionally, on the website you can:

- Keep up to date – when there are important changes to our publications, we will post updates on-line.

- Publications – the website contains hundreds of articles on Real Estate, everyday Life, and the Environment, written by Pierre Mouchette and available for free. There you will find more Books, Booklets, How-to-Articles, Guides and much, much more.

CONCENTRATED ANIMAL FEEDING OPERATIONS

Contents

Chapter 1   Meat ....- 6 -
   Meat ....- 7 -
      What is Meat? ....- 7 -
      Popular Meats ....- 7 -
      Which Type of Meat is Healthiest ....- 7 -
      Categories of Meat ....- 8 -
Chapter 2   Meat and Consumption ....- 9 -
   Factory Farms ....- 10 -
   About Factory Farming, People, and The Environment ....- 13 -
   About Factory Farming and Human Health ....- 15 -
   About What Is Fed to Animals on Factory Farms ....- 16 -
   About Factory Farm Animal Diseases ....- 17 -
Chapter 3   Shopping Smart ....- 20 -
   Shopping Smart ....- 21 -
   Humane Labeling ....- 22 -
APPENDIX A ....- 25 -
     GLOSSARY ....- 26 -
APPENDIX B ....- 28 -
     Commonly Used Words ....- 29 -
APPENDIX C ....- 31 -
   Regulatory ....- 32 -
   Consumer Advocates ....- 35 -

Meat and Hominids Brain Development

Meat gave modern man's distant ancestors the brain power to make higher-level decisions. The modern human brain is two to three times larger than that of our closest relatives, chimpanzees. But to supply energy to metabolically demanding tissue, a distinct trade-off in energy allocation had to evolve. In 1992, researchers proposed that this gradual expansion of the **'ancestral brain'** was made possible by switching from a vegetative diet to a meat-rich, fat-rich diet.

As meat became a dietary staple, the gut shortened, and the brain no longer needed to rely on fuel from muscle and fat stores in the body. A shorter gut requires less energy than the lengthy gut of herbivores. Drawing on the extra energy resources from a fatty diet, and a shorter gut, the brain could develop and grow.

It was the regular consumption of meat that is thought to have triggered major changes in the human lineage, the genus Homo, with this high-energy food supporting large brains.

CONCENTRATED ANIMAL FEEDING OPERATIONS

Chapter 1   Meat

CONCENTRATED ANIMAL FEEDING OPERATIONS

Meat

What is Meat?
Meat is animal flesh that is eaten as food. The advent of civilization allowed for the domestication of animals which eventually led to their use in meat production on an industrial scale.

Meat is composed of the muscle tissue of an animal, consisting of 75% water, 20% protein, and 5% fat carbohydrates, and assorted proteins. Muscles are made of bundles of cells called fibers. Unrefrigerated meat will spoil or rot within hours or days as a result of infection with, and decomposition by bacteria and fungi.

Vegetarians and vegans may abstain from eating meat because of concerns about the ethics of eating meat, environmental effects of meat production, or nutritional effects of consumption.

Popular Meats
There are many different types of meat, and all have been part of the human diet for thousands of years. Meat offers excellent nutritional value and provides a good range of essential nutrients. Some of the most sought-after meats are: Beef; Chicken; Duck; Goose; Lamb and Mutton; Pheasant; Pork; Rabbit; Turkey and Venison.

Which Type of Meat is Healthiest?
There is no single meat that is **'healthier'** than another. But there are a variety of factors to consider which include the nutrient profile, taste, and affordability. It is best to mix and match food choices, which can help to attain a greater range of nutrients.

- **Organ Meat** – these are among the most nutrient-dense of all foods. Although they are not as popular as they once were, foods like beef liver and kidneys are full of essential nutrients.

CONCENTRATED ANIMAL FEEDING OPERATIONS

Categories of Meat
Any meat you buy can be placed into one of several categories.

- **White meat** - as the name indicates, has a light color. Usually, it comes from a bird. The most common examples are chicken and turkey. Others include duck, goose, pheasant, and quail.

- **Red meat** - this type of meat can also be identified from its color, which in this case is reddish owing to the presents of myoglobin, a protein which is rich in iron. Examples of red meat include beef, pork, veal, goat, lamb, bison, venison, and elk.

- **Processed meat** - this is any type of meat (white or red) which has been extensively processed, using any number of modifications, including seasoning, drying, salting, smoking, curing, or the addition of preservatives.

- **Fish** - although some people do not consider it **'meat,'** it is the flesh of an animal.

The emphasis of this book is on those animals that are raised in the United States in a concentrated feeding operation.

CONCENTRATED ANIMAL FEEDING OPERATIONS

Chapter 2 Meat and Consumption

CONCENTRATED ANIMAL FEEDING OPERATIONS

Factory Farms

Commonly referred to as **'factory farms,' Concentrated Animal Feeding Operations (CAFO)s,** are animal producing operations that have become a common part of today's agricultural industry. They provide most of the **'food animals'** that Americans eat.

CAFOs are large **Animal Feeding Operations (AFO)** which congregate animals on a small land area. Feed is brought to the animals rather than the animals grazing or otherwise seeking feed in pastures, fields, or on rangeland.

In animal husbandry, a Concentrated Animal Feeding Operation (CAFO), as defined by the United States Department of Agriculture (USDA), is an intensive Animal Feeding Operation (AFO) in which over 1000 animal units are confined for over 45 days a year.

An animal unit is the equivalent of 1,000 pounds of live animal weight. A thousand animal units equates to 1,000 cattle, 700 cows used for dairy purposes, 2,500 pigs weighing more than 55 lbs., 125,000 chickens, or 82,000 egg laying hens or pullets.

There is no defining line between family farms (small farms) and CAFO farms. Many farms that are regulated as CAFOs are family owned and operated.

CONCENTRATED ANIMAL FEEDING OPERATIONS

The EPA has delineated three categories of CAFOs.

ANIMAL	LARGE	MEDIUM	SMALL
Cattle or cow/calf pairs	1,000 or more	300 - 999	less than 300
Mature dairy cattle	700 or more	200 - 699	less than 200
Turkeys	55,000 or more	16,500 – 54,999	less than 16,500
Laying Hens or Broilers	30,000 or more	9,000 – 29,999	less than 9,000
Chickens other than Laying Hens	125,000 or more	37,500–124,999	less than 37,500
Laying Hens	82,000 or more	25,000–81,999	less than 25,000

The categorization of CAFOs affects whether a facility is subject to regulation under the Clean Water Act (CWA), according to the 2008 rule adopted by the EPA.

- **Large CAFOs** - are automatically subject to EPA regulation.

- **Medium CAFOs** - must also meet one of two **'method of discharge'** criteria to be defined as a CAFO (or may be designated as such).

- **Small CAFOs** - can only be made subject to EPA regulations on a case-by-case basis. A small CAFO will also be designated a CAFO for purposes of the CWA if it discharges pollutants into waterways through a man-made conveyance such as a road, ditch, or pipe. Alternatively, a small CAFO may be designated an ordinary animal feeding operation (AFO) once its animal waste management system is certified at the site.

CONCENTRATED ANIMAL FEEDING OPERATIONS

Note: Because of continuous changes in the U.S. Animal Production Industry, where the number of operations are decreasing, and overall production is increasing. CAFOs are increasing in size and generating more waste, which requires disposal over more limited areas.

The environmental impact on surface waters has alarmed regulators and the public, with new regulations being developed to protect surface water quality. Although certain CAFO wastes have value as nutrient sources for plants, they can also contain pathogens, heavy metals, antibiotics, and hormones. The new regulations mandate that CAFOs have site specific Nutrient Management Plans (NMPs), which are one of the few risk-management tools available for protection of ground water quality following land application of CAFO wastes.

CONCENTRATED ANIMAL FEEDING OPERATIONS

About Factory Farming, People, and The Environment

Within the United States, there are more than nine billion animals raised and slaughtered for human consumption each year. This concentrated farming puts an incredible strain on natural resources such as land, water, and fossil fuel. Factory farms yield a small amount of meat, dairy, and eggs for their input, and in return produce staggering quantities of waste and greenhouse gases, thereby polluting land, air, and water in addition to contributing to climate change.

Factory farms:

- Generate more than 1 million tons of manure per day, which is three times the amount generated by the country's human population.

- Typically store animal waste in huge, open-air lagoons, which are prone to leaks and spills, which can contaminate a community's water. When the lagoons reach capacity, farmers will often apply manure to surrounding areas rather than pay to have the waste transported off-site. According to the USDA, animal waste can contaminate water supplies, emit harmful greenhouse gases, and hydrogen sulfide into the atmosphere when over-applied to land.

- Confined animals contribute to the spread of disease. To protect the animals and to also promote faster growth, producers feed the animals antibiotics. These antibiotics end up in their urine and manure and may contaminate waterways and crops which are ingested by humans.

FYI – in addition to watering the crops that farm animals eat, providing drinking water for the animals, cleaning the filth in factory farms and slaughterhouses, the animal agriculture industry has a huge impact on the nations water supply. (e.g., to produce one pound of beef it takes an estimated 1,581 gallons of water).

CONCENTRATED ANIMAL FEEDING OPERATIONS

People working at factory farms and those living near the farms are known to:

- Have an increase in respiratory, neurobehavioral, and mental illnesses.

- Evidence suggests that living near a factory farm compromises the residents' overall quality of life. Residents in towns near these farms are often forced to keep their windows closed and remain indoors due to foul odors.

CONCENTRATED ANIMAL FEEDING OPERATIONS

About Factory Farming and Human Health

Because of animal feeds, hormones, and the antibiotics used on factory farms, human populations are at risk for chronic disease, obesity, drug-resistant bacteria, in addition to creating a threat of major zoonotic disease outbreaks.

- **The Centers for Disease Control and Prevention (CDC),** states that animal products are the primary source of saturated fat in the American diet. Saturated fat has been linked to heart disease and obesity. Studies have shown that the unnatural feeds used to promote growth in animals on factory farms increase the saturated fat content of meat.

- Cows in the dairy industry can be given growth hormones in order to increase their milk production. Once their productivity declines, these cows are slaughtered for beef. Growth hormones commonly used by the U.S. dairy industry have been shown to significantly increase the risk of breast, prostate, and colon cancer in beef consumers.
  NOTE: Producers are not required to list the use of hormones on product labels.

- Antibiotics are used on factory farms to increase the growth rate in animals. Today, an estimated 70 percent of the antibiotics used in the U.S. are given to farm animals for non-therapeutic purposes. Using antibiotics in this way can lead to drug-resistant bacteria, and as a result certain bacterial infection have already become or are on their way to becoming untreatable in humans. If you want to know more about what drugs are fed to U.S. animals click here.

- Poor sanitation and waste management on factory farms and the poor management of animal waste can lead to the contamination of the food supply by bacteria such as E. coli and salmonella.

- Some diseases, such as H1N1 (swine flu) and avian flu, are communicable from animals to humans. These **'zoonotic diseases'** have the potential to become pandemics.

CONCENTRATED ANIMAL FEEDING OPERATIONS

About What Is Fed to Animals on Factory Farms

All factories are constantly searching for ways to cut their costs. To save money, factory farms have redefined what constitutes animal feed, with little consideration of what is best for the animals or for human health. As a result, many of the ingredients used in feed these days are not the kind of food the animals are designed by nature to eat. Some of the items (legally) that these animals are being fed are:

- Diseased Animals.
- Drugs and Chemicals.
- Feathers, Hair, Skin, Hooves, and Blood.
- Manure and Other Animal Waste.
- Plastics.
- Unhealthy Amounts of Grains.

With the appearance of **'mad cow disease'** in the 1970's (aka bovine spongiform encephalopathy or BSE), attention focused on the safety of feeding rendered cattle to cattle. Since then, the U.S. government has taken some action to restrict the parts of cattle that can be fed back to cattle.

Most animals need roughage to move food through their digestive systems. But instead of using plant-based roughage, animal factories often turn to pellets made from plastics to compensate for the lack of natural fiber in the factory feed.

If you are interested in reading more on what may be fed to the animals that you eat, click here.

Organic Agriculture prohibits the type of industrial agriculture feeding practices described above. This is one reason why millions of health and humane-minded consumers are switching to organic foods.

CONCENTRATED ANIMAL FEEDING OPERATIONS

About Factory Farm Animal Diseases

Zoonoses are infectious diseases caused by a pathogen (bacteria, viruses, parasites, etc.), that are transferred between species. For example, from animals to humans where modern industrial farming practices can turn health issues that were once benign into real concerns, due to their creation of perfect conditions for the proliferation of super bugs. The stress and unsanitary conditions of CAFOs weaken animals' immune systems and:

- Makes them more susceptible to infection.
- Overcrowding allows disease to spread quickly and easily; and over time, antibiotics can cause resistant strains of bacteria to evolve.

Note: these conditions, combined with a lack of diversification, create a petri dish for dangerous diseases.

Escherichia coli (E. coli) – this is a bacterium that normally lives in the intestines of healthy people and animals. Most varieties of E. coli are harmless or cause brief diarrhea. But some strains, such as E. coli O157:H7, can cause severe abdominal cramps, bloody diarrhea, and vomiting.

In cattle, mild strains of the bacteria have always been present in their stomachs, but the introduction of a grain-based diet changed this when the cattle's digestives systems became more acidic in order to tolerate the higher quantity of grain. As a result, more harmful acid-resistant strains of E. coli, like the infamous O157:H7, evolved to survive. This is the dangerous strain that has found its way into our water, produce, and meat in recent years.

The most common way to acquire an E. coli infection is by eating contaminated food, such as:

- **Beef** - when cattle are slaughtered and processed, E. coli bacteria in their intestines can get on the meat.

CONCENTRATED ANIMAL FEEDING OPERATIONS

- **Unpasteurized milk** - E. coli bacteria on a cow's udder or on milking equipment can get into raw milk.

Contaminated water - human and animal feces may pollute ground and surface water, including streams, rivers, lakes, and water used to irrigate crops. Although public water systems use chlorine, ultraviolet light, or ozone to kill E. coli, some outbreaks have been linked to contaminated municipal water supplies.

- **Fresh produce** - runoff from cattle farms can contaminate fields where fresh produce is grown.

Methicillin-resistant Styphylococcus aureus (MRSA) - is another bacterium that, thanks in part to **'factory farming,'** is popping up more than ever before. MRSA can be spread by human or animal carriers. It is abundant in our environment and its resistance to antibiotics can make it difficult to treat. No real research has been conducted on the presence of MRSA on animals in the U.S., but European studies show a **'strong causal link'** between MRSA and factory pig farms.

Campylobacter and Salmonella – a February 23, 1998 report by Consumer Reports stated that:

- **Campylobactor** - a foodborne illness that is usually found on poultry can be found on 63 percent of chicken sold in supermarkets. This infectious intestinal disease causes diarrhea, nausea, fever, and abdominal pain. They also noted that the CDC says the disease is becoming increasingly drug resistant.

- **Salmonella** - a similar but rarer bacterium is also becoming increasingly antibiotic-resistant as well.

Fortunately, these microbes can be killed by proper cooking.

CONCENTRATED ANIMAL FEEDING OPERATIONS

Mad cow disease - while much rarer than infectious bacteria, **Bovine Spongiform Encephalopathy (BSE)** can also be attributed to **modern factory farming practices.** Mad cow disease first appeared in the 1980s as a result of offal, a mixture of the organs and entrails of butchered cattle, in feed. Farmers quickly learned that **'cannibalism'** would cause infectious neurodegenerative diseases in livestock.

A 2003 report published by the World Health Organization explains: BSE is clearly linked to the practice of recycling bovine carcasses to recover **'meat and bone meal protein,'** and then feeding this protein back to other cattle. If cattle are not being fed protein derived from the carcasses of ruminants (cattle, sheep, and goats), there is no risk of BSE.

Obesity – because of government subsidies, the production of corn, corn syrup, and corn-based processed foods are attractive to farmers. Additionally, these products can cause a myriad of health issues and increase the fat content of conventionally produced beef.

Chapter 3 Shopping Smart

CONCENTRATED ANIMAL FEEDING OPERATIONS

Shopping Smart

Stay Away from Hormones
Livestock animals may be pumped full of estrogen, testosterone, progesterone, and other hormones to boost production. Many health conditions which are pervasive in today's world involve hormonal imbalances.

These conditions are not well understood now, but it is likely that the presence of hormones in meats would be a contributing factor to some of these imbalances. For this reason, when you are shopping for meats, you should look on the packaging for labels that indicate that the animals were not given extra hormones. Many livestock producers add hormones to their stock. This is done to increase productivity. Unfortunately, this practice may have consequences for human health. Avoid meats with added hormones.

Ethical Meat Eating
While not a nutritional concern, it is worth taking a moment to mention the health and well-being of animals as well as the planet.

- If you are going to eat meats, you should shop with ethics in mind, and choose meat which has been humanely raised with a low environmental impact.

- Animals which are confined have higher ratios of polyunsaturated fats, which are bad for your health.

- Meat which has been genetically modified may have unpredictable effects on your body.

- There is also some (albeit minimal) concern that meat injected with antibiotics could contribute to the spread of disease among human beings.

From an ethical standpoint, you should stay away from factory farmed meat, and choose free range organic meat. Doing so may also have nutritional benefits.

CONCENTRATED ANIMAL FEEDING OPERATIONS

Humane Labeling

Today, many people question if buying meat, milk, and eggs with labels such **as 'cage-free,' 'grass-fed,' or 'free-range'** is a humane option. They are concerned about where their food comes from, and genuinely want to make better choices. Unfortunately, these labels can be misleading and are not a guarantee of humane treatment.

Chicken

- **Cage-free hens** are subject to many of the cruelties inherent to battery-cage systems. For instance, cage-free producers typically purchase hens from hatcheries, where male egg-type chickens are considered useless and killed at birth because they will not lay eggs and will not grow as large as chickens bred for meat. Hatcheries kill 260 million male chicks each year.

- Just like caged hens, **cage-free hens suffer debeaking,** in which a portion of the beak is amputated without pain relief. Also, like caged hens, cage-free layers are kept only for a few years, until their productivity begins to decline. Then they are typically shipped to industrial slaughterhouses. Since poultry animals are excluded from the federal **Humane Slaughter Act,** packing plants are not required to render these animals' unconscious before slaughter.

- Though **cage-free hens** are not confined to battery cages, they may still be packed by the thousands into poorly ventilated, windowless warehouses. Undercover investigations have revealed cage-free hens commonly living indoors, packed so tightly that they can barely move or spread their wings.

- **USDA regulations** do not specify the amount, duration, or quality of outdoor access provided to free-range animals. This means that a warehouse with thousands of free-range hens could have a single door leading to a small, enclosed outdoor area that hens would have to struggle to access.

- Grass-fed labels indicate that animals receive most of their nutrients from grass throughout their life, but USDA grass-fed stipulations do not limit the use of antibiotics, hormones, or pesticides, all of which are harmful to the environment and human health.

Cows

- An organic dairy may be free of antibiotics and hormones, but it is not free of cruelty. Because cows produce milk only when pregnant or nursing, all dairy farms subject their cows to a relentless cycle of impregnation and birth. Their babies are taken away immediately, so that the milk can be collected for human use. Male calves, since they are of no use to the dairy industry, are sold for beef or veal. When a cow's milk production declines at an average of less than five years, she too is slaughtered for meat.

- Investigations have shown that some organic milk producers keep cows confined indoors much of the time. Because the requirements for the organic label prohibit the use of many medicines, producers frequently allow cows to languish with ailments that otherwise could easily be treated.

Action Tips for Buying Nutritious Meat
The following tips should help you shop for nutritious meat:

- Buy both red and white meat. But try and avoid processed meat when you can.

- Look for meat which has been raised without hormones and antibiotics.

- Do not buy factory farmed meat. Look for free range meat instead. Animals that can have space to roam around and live humanely have a healthier fat profile.

- If you are shopping for organic meat, look for the **USDA Organic label** so that you know what you are getting.

- A variety of meats can provide you with a rich abundance of nutrition.

CONCENTRATED ANIMAL FEEDING OPERATIONS

- A good go-to meat is beef, which has a better fat profile than pork or chicken.

- You do not always have to go for the leanest cuts of meats. If you are on a low-carb diet, you need fat for energy. But the quality of the fat is important.

- Fish is a fantastic choice when it comes to increasing your omega-3 fatty acid intake.

CONCENTRATED ANIMAL FEEDING OPERATIONS

APPENDIX A

GLOSSARY

Organic - these are products that come from animals that are not given any antibiotics or growth hormones and plants that do not use conventional pesticides (fertilizers made with synthetic ingredients, bioengineering or radiation).

To be organic an official certifier has to inspect the farm or product to verify that all guidelines are followed. In addition, there are standards for the handling and processing of these products.

There are currently a few different levels of organic claims:

- **100% Organic** - products that are completely organic or made of only organic ingredients.

- **Organic** - products with at least 95% of their ingredients being organic.

- **Made with Organic Ingredients** – these are products with at least 70% of their ingredients being certified organic.

Natural - one of the least understood and the most contested claim. Consumers associate it with something good, but there is no formal definition from the FDA, or any association of food producers. The FDA requires labeling information to be **"truthful and not misleading,"** so 'natural' should not be used arbitrarily.

The terminology 'natural' means being minimally processed and not containing added color, artificial flavor, or synthetic substances. The USDA defines it, by stating that natural meat, poultry, and egg products be minimally processed and contain no artificial ingredients. It does not, include any standards for agricultural practices. If using 'natural' on a label, a statement must accompany it explaining the meaning of the term (e.g., no artificial ingredients; minimally processed). 'Natural' is not permitted in a product's ingredient list except in terms like "natural flavorings".

CONCENTRATED ANIMAL FEEDING OPERATIONS

Vegan - employs a clear definition in the vegan and its general community but does not have a formal definition from the **FDA, USDA, or FTC** for the purposes of labeling. Here the term usage means that the product does not contain ingredients of animal origin, including milk, eggs, honey, and gelatin.

Although not required, there are various certification programs that may establish more trust from consumers. These certifications are stricter than the above definition of vegan and may require that no animal testing has been done on any ingredients as well as some additional levels of scrutiny.

Raw - a newer term that occasionally has been seen on food labels and in food marketing. It is currently not governed by the **FDA or USDA,** or any other governing body.
Note: the caveat here is that any food claiming to be Raw, must be truthful and not misleading, otherwise the FDA can act against a false claim.

Kosher - these foods must be prepared from specific foods, by specific people and equipment, in a specific manner, and certified by one of the many Kosher agencies.

Note: different Kosher certification agencies follow different standards, with some more and others less strict. Different certification and symbols mean different things, so it is important verify and get the correct certification. Kosher means that foods do not use pork products, meat and dairy cannot be combined, slaughter must be performed in a specific manner, and food must be produced with kosher utensils and machinery that are not used to make non-kosher foods or used for both meat and dairy products.

CONCENTRATED ANIMAL FEEDING OPERATIONS

APPENDIX B

CONCENTRATED ANIMAL FEEDING OPERATIONS

Commonly Used Words

Grass Fed - Definition by:
U.S. Department of Agriculture- Food Safety and inspection Service (FSIS)

- The meat must come from animals that have never been given grain and have access to pasture during the grazing season, although the farms are not required to be inspected by the agency.

- The animal can still be raised with antibiotics or hormones.

Note: partial grass-fed claims, such as 85-percent grass-fed, on beef are permitted, but they are meaningless. All cattle spend the first part of their lives eating grass or hay; some are fed grain to make them grow faster and larger before slaughter. So, there is little difference between a partially grass-fed animal and a conventionally fed one. In addition, these animals may not have continuous access to pasture and spend a portion of their lives confined to a feedlot.

Humanely Raised
This term has no official definition, and it is not verified either by USDA or any independent organization. To be certain the meat you buy comes from animals that are humanely raised, look for the **Animal Welfare Approved seal, a GAP 1-5+ label, or the Certified Humane seal.**

The **USDA Organic seal** has some animal welfare standards, such as adequate space, but not to the same degree as other animal welfare labels.

A "NO ANTIBIOTIC" or "RAISED WITHOUT ANTIBIOTIC" claim should be reliable, but verification is not required. The meat producer can submit an affidavit to the USDA, but the agency does not inspect the farms. The label does not mean that hormones or other drugs were not used.

However, if you see the claim **"no growth promoting antibiotics,"** *it is an attempt to put one over on consumers.* The FDA has asked drug companies to change the labels on antibiotics used in animals to indicate that they are not for growth promotion. But they can still be used **'to ensure animal health,'** or to **'prevent or control disease.'** That means the practice of giving animals low doses of antibiotics throughout their lives can continue, just under another name, doing little if anything to help control the development of antibiotic resistant bacteria.

While it may be true that no growth promoting antibiotics were used, antibiotics could have been used for disease prevention. Sick animals should be treated with antibiotics, and the low doses that are given to animals regularly to prevent disease destroy only some bacteria. The few hardy survivors are excreted in manure, where they multiply, eventually leading to colonies of more and more indestructible superbugs.

APPENDIX C

CONCENTRATED ANIMAL FEEDING OPERATIONS

Regulatory

The Environmental Protection Agency (EPA)
This is an agency of the federal government of the United States which was created to protect human health and the environment by writing and enforcing regulations based on laws passed by Congress. The EPA has the responsibility of maintaining and enforcing national standards under a variety of environmental laws, in consultation with state, tribal, and local governments.

Environmental Protection Agency
1200 Pennsylvania Ave, N.W.
Washington, DC 20460

https://www.epa.gov/

The United States Department of Health and Human Services (HHS)
The FDA is a federal agency of the United States Department of Health and Human Services.

U.S. Food and Drug Administration
10903 New Hampshire Avenue
Silver Spring, MD 20993
1-888-INFO-FDA (1-888-463-6332)

https://www.fda.gov/

CONCENTRATED ANIMAL FEEDING OPERATIONS

The Food and Drug Administration (FDA)
The FDA is a federal agency of the United States Department of Health and Human Services.

U.S. Food and Drug Administration
10903 New Hampshire Avenue
Silver Spring, MD 20993
1-888-INFO-FDA (1-888-463-6332)

https://www.fda.gov/

U.S. Department of Agriculture (USDA) Organic
USDA certified organic foods are grown and processed according to federal guidelines addressing, soil quality, animal raising practices, pest and weed control, and the use of additives. Organic producers rely on natural substances and physical, mechanical, or biologically based farming methods to the fullest extent possible.

Regulations for organic meat require that animals are raised in living conditions accommodating their natural behaviors (the ability to graze on pasture), fed 100% organic feed and forage, and not administered antibiotics or hormones.

Additional Resources:

- Fact Sheet: What is Organic?
- Guide for Organic Crop Producers
- Guide for Organic Livestock Producers
- Guide for Organic Processors
- Guide to Organic Certification

https://www.usda.gov/topics/organic

CONCENTRATED ANIMAL FEEDING OPERATIONS

U.S. Department of Agriculture – Food Safety and Inspection Service (FSIS)

USDA's Food Safety and Inspection Service (FSIS) is responsible for ensuring the safety and wholesomeness of meat, poultry, and processed egg products and ensures that it is accurately labeled.

- FSIS enforces the Federal Meat Inspection Act (FMIA), the Poultry Products Inspection Act (PPIA), and the Egg Products Inspection Act. These laws require Federal inspection and regulation of meat, poultry, and processed egg products prepared for distribution in commerce for use as human food. It also verifies compliance with the Humane Methods of Slaughter Act for livestock. This statute is enforced through the FMIA.

Food Safety and Inspection Service
U.S. Department of Agriculture
1400 Independence Ave., S.W.
Washington, DC 20250-3700

(202) 720-9113

https://www.fsis.usda.gov/wps/portal/fsis/home

Consumer Advocates

The Environmental Working Group (EWG)
EWG is an independent consumer-powering organization that is dedicated to protecting human health and the environment. Their mission is to empower people to live healthier lives in a healthier environment. EWG is a 501(c)(3) nonprofit corporation.

HEADQUARTERS
1436 U Street NW, Suite 100
Washington, DC 20009

(202) 667-6982

https://www.ewg.org/

People for the Ethical Treatment of Animals (PETA)
People for the Ethical Treatment of Animals is a animal rights organization, that focuses its attention on four areas in which the largest numbers of animals suffer the most intensely for the longest periods of time: in laboratories, in the food industry, in the clothing trade, and in the entertainment industry.

PETA works through public education, cruelty investigations, research, animal rescue, legislation, special events, celebrity involvement, and protest campaigns.

PETA is a nonprofit, tax-exempt 501(c)(3) corporation

People for the Ethical Treatment of Animals
501 Front Street
Norfolk, VA 23510
757-622-PETA (7382)
https://www.peta.org/

CONCENTRATED ANIMAL FEEDING OPERATIONS

WE HAVE YOU COVERED

At Real Property Experts, we publish for you! At home, at work, or just taking a break we have the solution for you. Our publications are available in:

- **Paperback.**
- **PDF (Portable Document Format).**
- **EPUB (open standard format).**
- **AZW3 (Amazon Kindle eReader).**
- **IBA (Apple iBooks).**

Yes, we have you covered!

CONCENTRATED ANIMAL FEEDING OPERATIONS

AFTERWORD

Thank you for reading

**WHAT TO KNOW ABOUT
CONCENTRATED ANIMAL FEEDING OPERATIONS**

We hope you enjoyed this Life Knowledge Publication

Thank you again valued reader,
and we hope to meet you again on another book.

ABOUT THE AUTHOR

Pierre Mouchette is the Founder and CEO of Real Property Experts LLC. He is a graduate of New York University, with a Master's in Business Administration, a Certificate in Real Estate Law - Fairfield University - CT, Graduate of the Realtors Institute – CT, and held licensing as a Real Estate Broker, and a Mortgage Broker.

Pierre is currently authoring Books, Booklets, How-to-Articles, and Guides in retirement. Pierre has an extensive background in real estate investment, business management and sales, supplemented by decades of hands-on-experience in building systems engineering, development, evaluation, and assorted analytical engineering studies.

Using background knowledge and experience, Pierre launched Real Property Experts in 2013 to help simplify real estate investing by connecting investors through innovative technology. In 2018, Pierre created THE SYNCHRONICITY INVESTOR a real estate website to facilitate providing world-class solutions for real estate investors and investment businesses.

Environmental Knowledge Publications

By Pierre Mouchette

HEALTH

Get Rid of The Stink – A Guide for Property Owners

PFAS – The Forever Chemical

WHAT TO KNOW ABOUT – Concentrated Animal Feeding Operations

NATURAL RESOURCES

WATER – Natures Holistic Medicine That's Vital For Life

www.ingramcontent.com/pod-product-compliance
Lightning Source LLC
Chambersburg PA
CBHW070904220526
45466CB00005B/2120